# CORN

by **GAIL GIBBONS**

Holiday House / New York

# To Wanda and Clayton

Special thanks to Becky Grube,
Horticultural Specialist at the University of New Hampshire,
Durham, New Hampshire.

Copyright © 2008 by Gail Gibbons
All Rights Reserved
Printed and Bound in March 2020 at Toppan Leefung, DongGuan City, China.
www.holidayhouse.com

7 9 10 8
Library of Congress Cataloging-in-Publication Data
Gibbons, Gail.
Corn / by Gail Gibbons.
p. cm.
ISBN 978-0-8234-2169-5 (hardcover)
ISBN 978-0-8234-2245-6 (pbk)

1. Corn—United States—Juvenile literature. 2. Corn
industry—United States—Juvenile literature. I. Title.
HD9049.C8U524 2008
633.1'50973—dc22
2007051632

Corn is so good to eat.

UNITED STATES

GULF OF MEXICO

CENTRAL AMERICA

MEXICO

PACIFIC OCEAN

MAYAN CIVILIZATION

The native peoples called corn MAIZE.

CULTIVATE means to grow plants or crops.

Corn is a grain that was cultivated thousands of years ago in what is now called Mexico and Central America. It was the major crop for the great Mayan civilization.

The Aztecs also had a great civilization and used corn in many ways to feed themselves and their animals.

The native peoples in what is now Canada and the United States also grew corn.

MASSACHUSETTS

ATLANTIC OCEAN

Plymouth

In 1620 people sailed from England to the Americas and came ashore at what is now Plymouth, Massachusetts. They were called Pilgrims. The winter was cold, and they had very little to eat.

In the spring local Native American Indians taught the Pilgrims how to grow corn.

The Pilgrims called this crop **INDIAN CORN.**

In the fall the Indian corn was fully grown.

The Pilgrims held a great feast celebrating their bountiful harvest.
The Indians joined them at this first Thanksgiving.

CORN PUDDING

CORN BREAD

COBS for fuel

HUSKS to stuff mattresses

POPCORN

CORN HUSK DOLLS

The Pilgrims learned to use corn in many different ways.

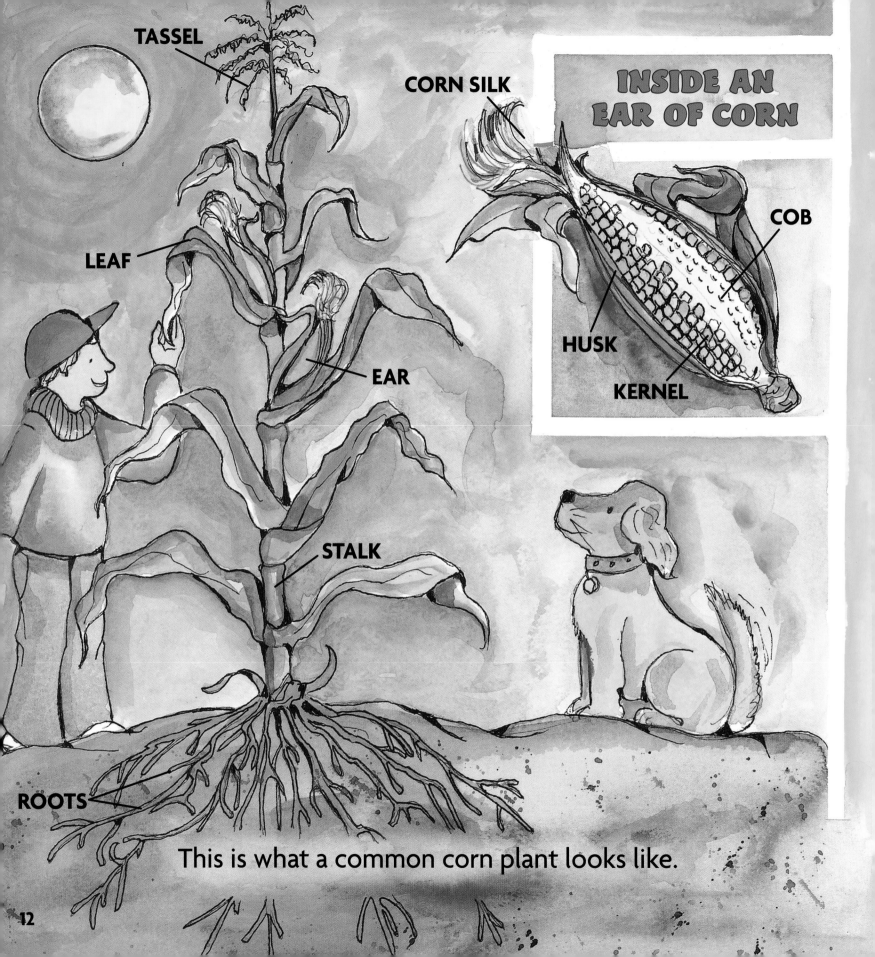

TASSEL

CORN SILK

**INSIDE AN EAR OF CORN**

LEAF

COB

HUSK

EAR

KERNEL

STALK

ROOTS

This is what a common corn plant looks like.

It is generally agreed that there are four different types of corn. Each type has many varieties.

# SWEET CORN

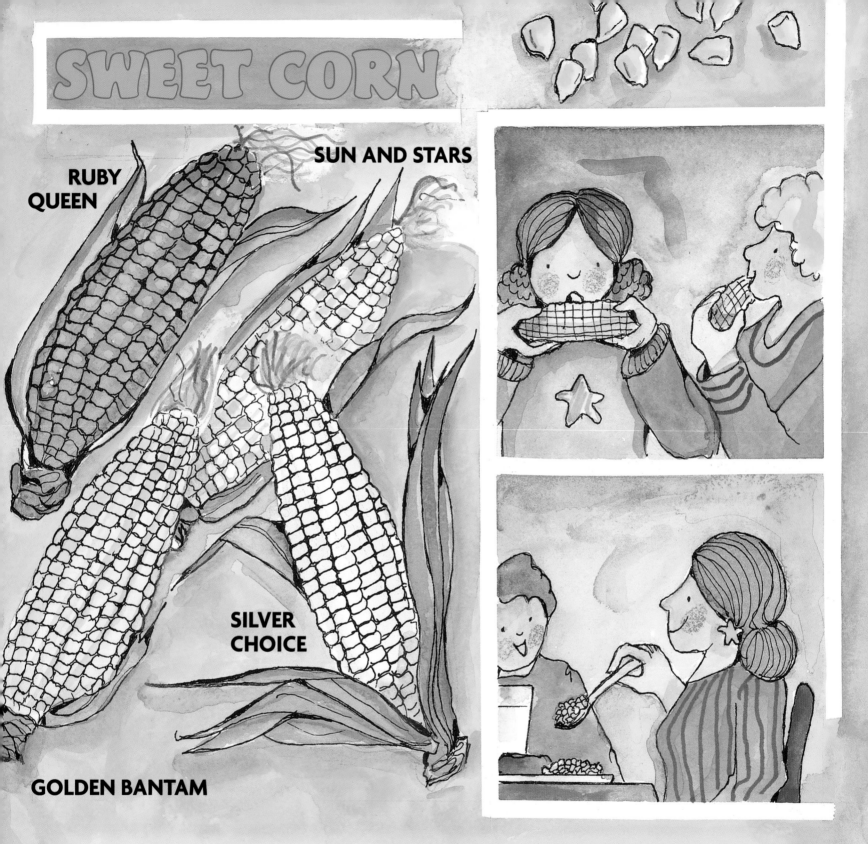

RUBY QUEEN

SUN AND STARS

SILVER CHOICE

GOLDEN BANTAM

Sweet corn is the most common corn that people eat. People love eating sweet corn because the kernels are soft, sweet, and juicy.

Sweet corn is harvested just before the kernels turn hard. All other types of corn are harvested after the kernels turn hard.

# POPCORN

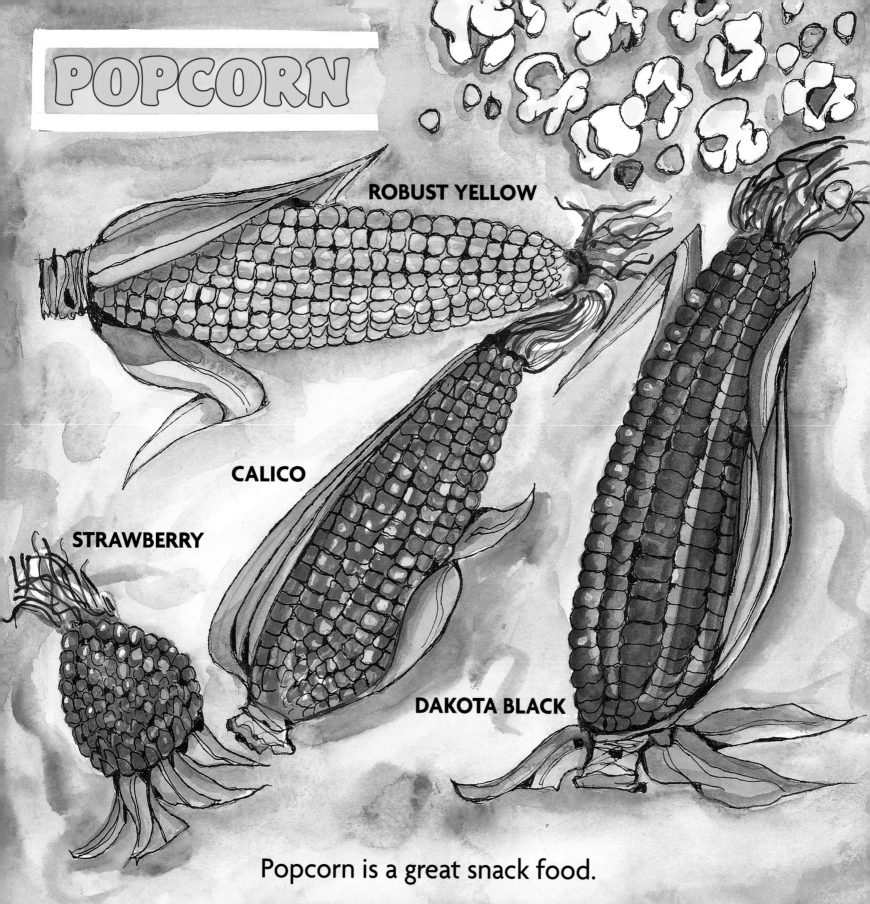

ROBUST YELLOW

CALICO

STRAWBERRY

DAKOTA BLACK

Popcorn is a great snack food.

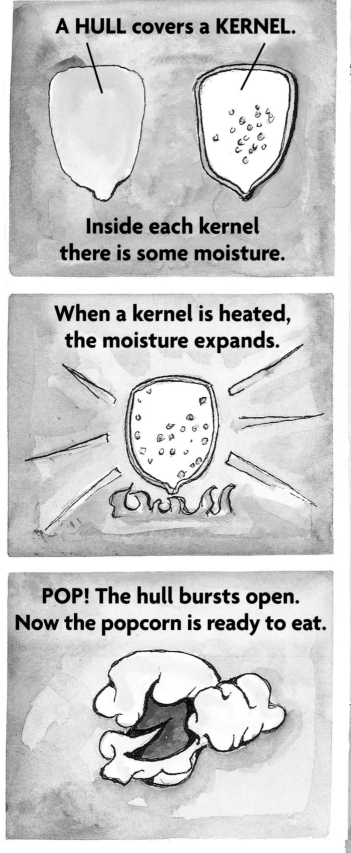

**A HULL covers a KERNEL.**

Inside each kernel
there is some moisture.

When a kernel is heated,
the moisture expands.

POP! The hull bursts open.
Now the popcorn is ready to eat.

# FLINT CORN

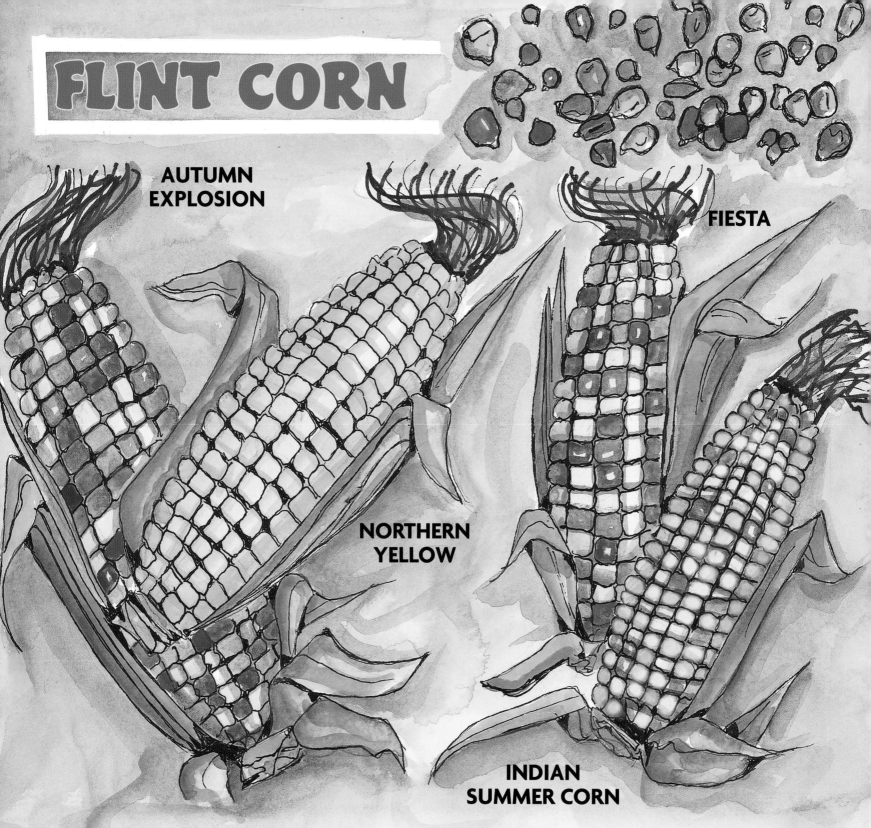

AUTUMN EXPLOSION

FIESTA

NORTHERN YELLOW

INDIAN SUMMER CORN

Flint corn is used in many foods we eat. It is used to feed animals too.

CEREAL

CORNMEAL

FALL DECORATIONS

GRITS

POLENTA

ANIMAL FEED

19

# DENT CORN

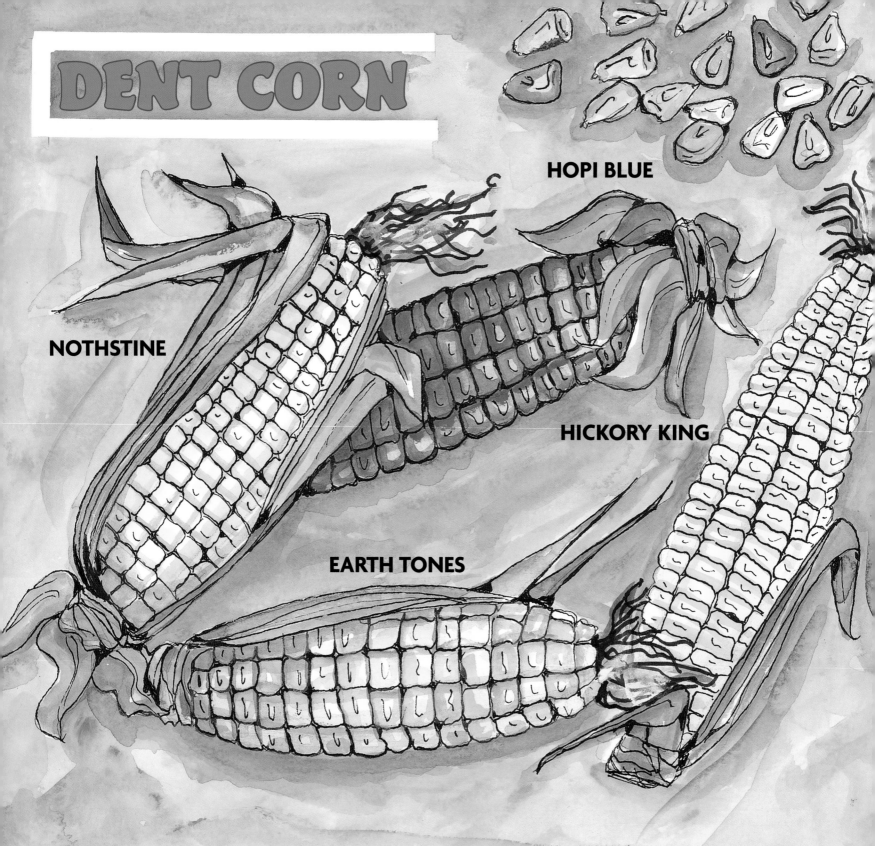

HOPI BLUE

NOTHSTINE

HICKORY KING

EARTH TONES

Dent corn is also used for many different kinds of foods.

CORN MUFFINS

FLOUR

CORN BREAD

CHIPS

ANIMAL FEED

TACOS

TORTILLAS

TAMALES

# PLANTING

KERNELS are corn seeds.

ROW PLANTER

PLOW

TRACTOR

A PLOW and ROW PLANTER are used to turn over the soil and plant kernels.

5 DAYS

4 WEEKS

8 WEEKS

A corn stalk begins to grow. Cobs covered by husks appear.

# POLLINATION

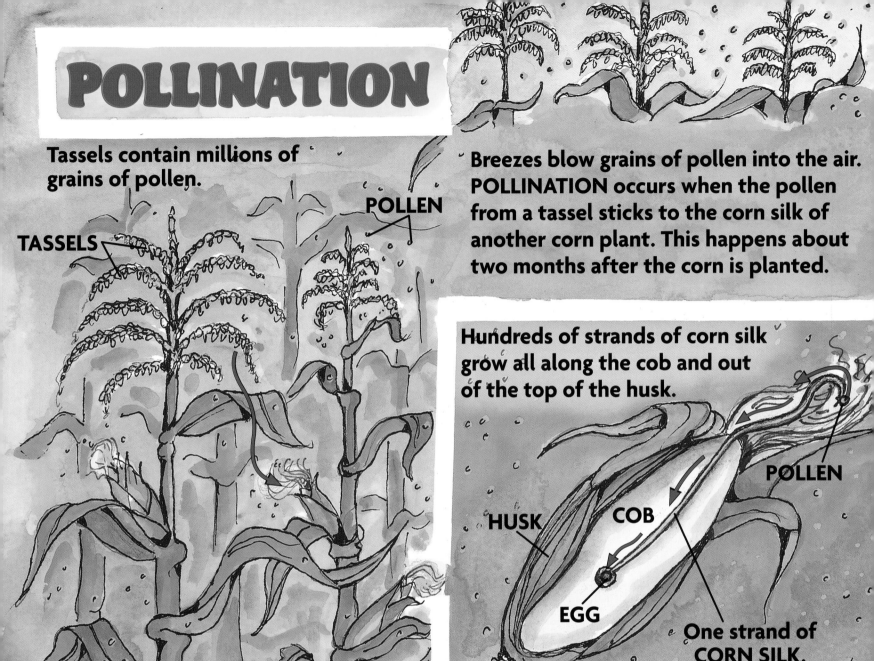

Tassels contain millions of grains of pollen.

**TASSELS**

**POLLEN**

Breezes blow grains of pollen into the air. POLLINATION occurs when the pollen from a tassel sticks to the corn silk of another corn plant. This happens about two months after the corn is planted.

Hundreds of strands of corn silk grow all along the cob and out of the top of the husk.

**POLLEN**

**HUSK**

**COB**

**EGG**

One strand of **CORN SILK.**

Each ear of corn has a great many corn silks. At the end of each corn silk is an egg that is attached to the cob. Pollen moves down each corn silk. When a grain of pollen and an egg join together, the egg is fertilized, and a kernel begins to grow. There is one corn silk and one egg for each kernel.

# HARVESTING

SWEET CORN is harvested before the silks turn brown and the kernels are still tender.

Three to four months after the corn has been planted, the corn silks begin to turn brown.

The average corn plant is about 8 feet (2.4 m) tall. The average ear is about 8 inches (20.3 cm) long.

This means the kernels are ripe and the corn is ready to be harvested.

# Large Industrial Farms
## PLANTING

On large farms a plow is used to turn over the topsoil.

TRACTOR

PLOW

A large row planter is used to plant the corn kernels.

TRACTOR

ROW PLANTER

# HARVESTING

**A CORN PICKER MACHINE** picks each ear of corn individually.

**EARS OF CORN**

**A CORN COMBINE MACHINE** picks the ears from the stalks, removes the husks, and then removes the kernels from the cobs.

**KERNELS**

**A CORN FORAGE HARVESTER** cuts up the whole plant into small pieces for silage (sye•lij).

**SILAGE**

This **SILO** is full of **SILAGE**.

Some people grow corn in their gardens and pick it by hand.

COWS

PIGS

POULTRY

Much of the corn grown is used to feed animals.

CORN ON THE COB

CANNED CORN

FROZEN CORN

NATURAL SWEETENER

CORN SYRUP

SALAD DRESSINGS

JAMS & JELLIES

FRUIT DRINKS    SOFT DRINKS

CORN CHIPS

MILLED FOR CORN FLOUR

FLOUR

TORTILLAS

CEREAL

CORN MUFFINS

CORN BREAD

SOAP

GLUE

CORN OIL FOR COOKING

OIL

STARCH

BABY POWDER

CORNSTARCH

PAINTS & DYES

CLOTH

MEDICINES

PAPER PRODUCTS

ETHANOL FOR FUEL

BIODEGRADABLE PLASTIC & PACKING MATERIALS

It's amazing how many ways corn can be used.

Corn can also be nutritious and delicious.

# CORN...CORN...CORN...

In the United States, the highest corn-producing states, known as the CORN BELT, are Illinois, Indiana, Iowa, Kansas, Minnesota, Missouri, Nebraska, Ohio, South Dakota, and Wisconsin.

Canada produces about 13 million tons (11.8 metric tons) of corn a year.

Corn varieties range from 3 feet (.9 m) to 20 feet (6 m) tall.

In Canada the provinces of Ontario and Quebec produce the most corn.

The tassel at the top of each cornstalk contains up to 25 million grains of pollen.

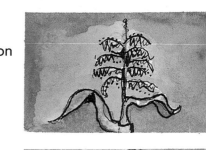

An acre (.405 hectares) of land may yield about 4 tons (3.6 metric tons) of corn a year.

The average cob has about 800 kernels.

When corn is distilled it produces alcohol that can be mixed with gasoline to make a fuel called ETHANOL.

The United States produces about 84 million tons (76.2 metric tons) of corn a year.

Corn is grown on every continent except Antarctica.

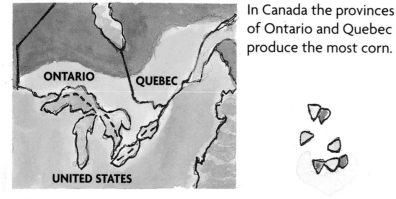

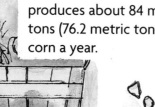

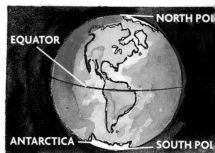